CW01261245

YOU AND YOUR CHILD
KITCHEN FUN

Ray Gibson
Illustrated by Sue Stitt, Simone Abel
and Graham Round 
Designed by Carol Law
Edited by Robyn Gee
Series editor: Jenny Tyler
Photography by Lesley Howling

This book provides parents and children with lots of easy, tasty and original ideas for things to cook together. There are sweets and savouries, including recipes for everyday dishes or for special occasions. Besides introducing children to some of the most basic cooking techniques and giving them fun and satisfaction, the activities in this book will also help to develop their ideas about size, shape, weight, measurement and time, broaden their vocabulary and give them early counting and reading opportunities.

First published in 1990 by Usborne Publishing Ltd, Usborne House, 83-85 Saffron Hill, London EC1N 8RT, England. Copyright © 1990 Usborne Publishing Ltd. The name Usborne and the device ♛ are Trade Marks of Usborne Publishing Ltd. All rights reserved. No part of this publication may be reproduced, stored in any form or by any means, electronic, mechanical, photocopying, recording, or otherwise, without the prior permission of the publisher. Printed in Belgium.

Juicy jellies

You will need:
- 3 jellies (1 green, 1 yellow, 1 other)
- ready roll icing
- food colouring
- flower sweets
- angelica
- fresh or canned fruit
- squirty cream

Jelly pond

Make up green and yellow jellies together, as directed on the packet, in a large mixing bowl. When cool refrigerate until beginning to set.

Cut pieces of icing off the block and colour them by rolling them in a few drops of food colouring. Leave some white.

Make fish, snakes and snails from the icing (see below). Press them firmly onto the inside of a glass or plastic bowl.

When the jelly is nearly set, pour it carefully into the glass bowl.*

Reeds made from angelica pressed into strips of icing.

When the jelly is firmly set, arrange some ducks, weeds, waterlilies and reeds on the top.

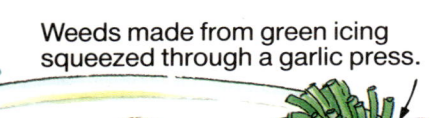

Weeds made from green icing squeezed through a garlic press.

Fish
Flatten a piece of icing. Cut out body and tail shapes. Press in an eye with a pencil covered in clingfilm. Press on some tiny spots.

Snakes
Roll long sausage shapes and press in eyes.

Ducks
Press two balls together, then pinch out a tail and add a beak.

Waterlilies
Flatten balls and shape them into leaves. Mark with a knife. Place flower sweets on top.

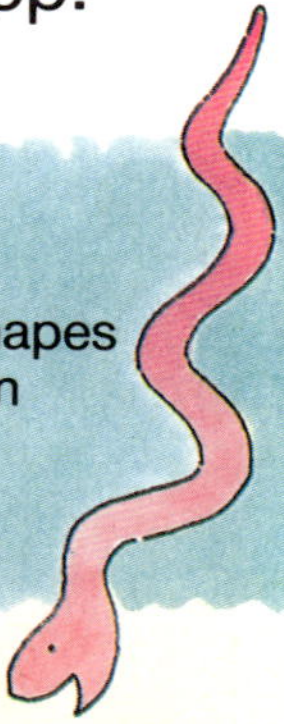

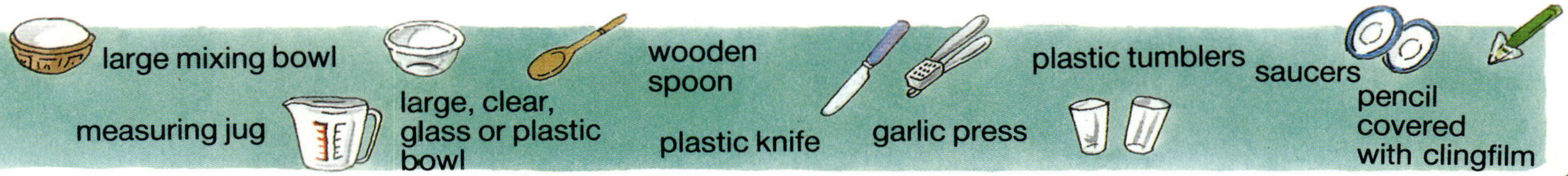

large mixing bowl · measuring jug · large, clear, glass or plastic bowl · wooden spoon · plastic knife · garlic press · plastic tumblers · saucers · pencil covered with clingfilm

Jelly wobblers

Make up a jelly with 75 ml less water than given in the instructions. Allow to cool but not set.

Peel, slice and de-seed fresh fruit, or drain canned fruit, and arrange in plastic tumblers.

Pour on the jelly and leave it to set in the fridge.

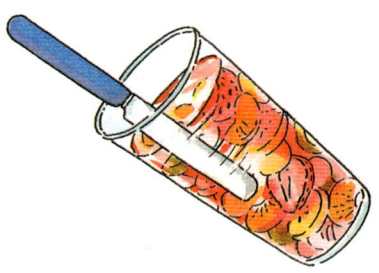

When they have set, ease round the sides of the jellies with a plastic knife.

Turn them out onto saucers and decorate the tops with cream and fruit.

Other ideas to try:

Monster in a lake
Roll a long, fat snake out of ready roll icing. Cut it into four sections.

Water babies
On a set jelly, arrange some icing "rocks" and stand jelly babies on them.
Add squirty cream for waves.

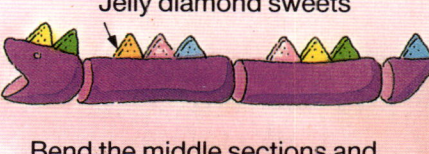

Jelly diamond sweets

Bend the middle sections and place them on a set jelly.

***Hint**
Don't pour liquid jelly over icing or it will start to dissolve.

3

Set oven to:
220°C   425°F
Gas mark 7

Fishy puffs

You will need: packet of puff pastry (thawed), 1 egg, lemon, parsley, flour, smoked mackerel or drained can of tuna

Press in lines.

Roll out the puff pastry thinly (about 2 mm deep) on a floured surface.

To make large fish cut round a side plate with a knife. For small fish use scone-cutters.

From the leftover pastry cut out tail shapes with a knife. Use a pen-top dipped in flour to cut out "spots".

Leave the edges uncovered.

Place the pastry circle on an oiled baking tray. Brush the edges with beaten egg.

Put some fish on one half of the pastry. Add a squeeze of lemon and some parsley.

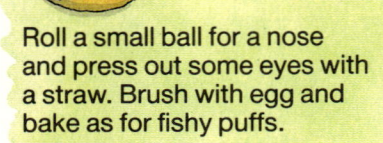

Fat bunnies

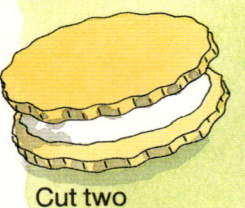

Use scone-cutters to make two circles. Put some filling on one circle and press the other circle over it.

Cut two fat cheeks with a bottle-top. Stick them on.

From another circle cut out two ears.

Roll a small ball for a nose and press out some eyes with a straw. Brush with egg and bake as for fishy puffs.

Fillings
• Cottage cheese with peas or honey.
• Triangle of processed cheese with a small slice of ham.

4

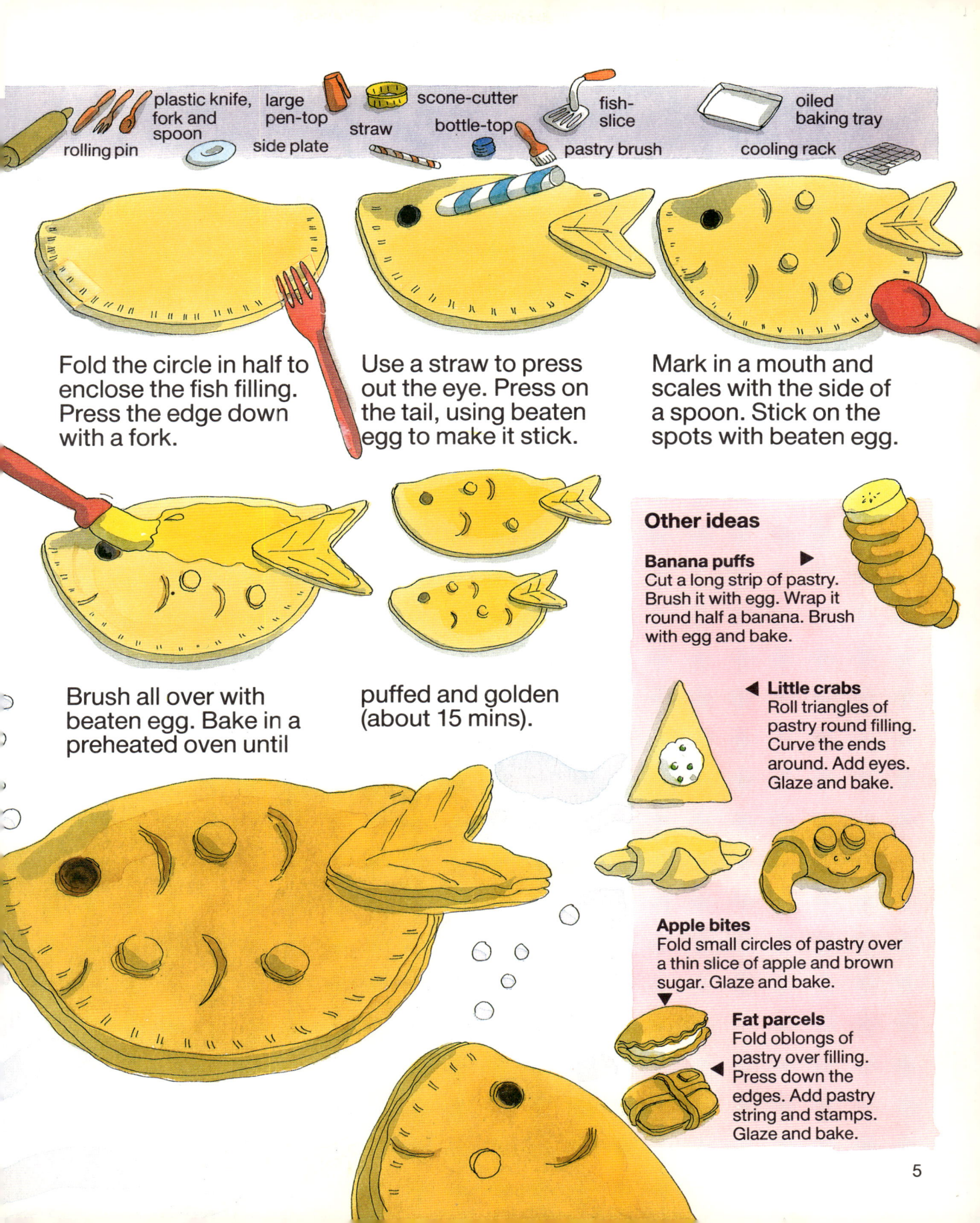

rolling pin — plastic knife, fork and spoon — large pen-top — side plate — straw — scone-cutter — bottle-top — fish-slice — pastry brush — oiled baking tray — cooling rack

Fold the circle in half to enclose the fish filling. Press the edge down with a fork.

Use a straw to press out the eye. Press on the tail, using beaten egg to make it stick.

Mark in a mouth and scales with the side of a spoon. Stick on the spots with beaten egg.

Brush all over with beaten egg. Bake in a preheated oven until puffed and golden (about 15 mins).

Other ideas

Banana puffs ▶
Cut a long strip of pastry. Brush it with egg. Wrap it round half a banana. Brush with egg and bake.

◀ **Little crabs**
Roll triangles of pastry round filling. Curve the ends around. Add eyes. Glaze and bake.

Apple bites
Fold small circles of pastry over a thin slice of apple and brown sugar. Glaze and bake.

Fat parcels
Fold oblongs of pastry over filling. Press down the edges. Add pastry string and stamps. Glaze and bake.

Set oven to: 200°C 400°F Gas mark 6

Valentine tarts

You will need:
- 100 g plain or self-raising flour
- pinch of salt
- 25 g margarine
- 25 g lard
- jam

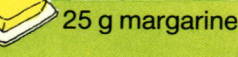

- 2 tablespoons cold water
- large mixing bowl
- plastic scone cutter
- knife
- teaspoon
- plastic bottle-top
- cooling rack
- greased bun tray

Mix the flour and salt in a large bowl. Cut up the fat and gently rub it in.

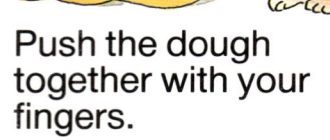

Stir in the water quickly with a knife.

Push the dough together with your fingers.

Roll out the dough on a floured board until it is about 3 mm thick. Cut out large circles with a scone cutter.

From the scraps cut out some small circles with a bottle-top and make them into hearts as shown.

Push in top edge, using clingfilm covered pencil.
Pinch lower edge into a point.
Flatten out gently with fingertips.

Press the large circles gently into a greased bun tray. Put a large teaspoon of jam in each one and place the hearts on top.

Bake for about 15 minutes in a preheated oven.

Hints
- Use a ball of dough to press the circles of pastry gently into the bun tray.
- Do not put too much jam in the tarts, or it may bubble over the edges.
- Allow the jam plenty of time to cool down, before touching or tasting the tarts.

Set oven to:
180°C 350°F
Gas mark 4

Duck on a lake cake

You will need: 1 quantity Victoria sponge cake mix (see p 32) — pink and green food colouring — jam — icing sugar

1 large bowl — 2 small bowls — 2 dessert spoons — greased cake tin (approx. 18 cm) — knife — breadknife — scissors — thick felt-tip pen — greaseproof paper — sieve — cooling rack

Make up your cake mixture in a large bowl (see page 32).

Put a third of the mixture into each small bowl. Leave a third in the large bowl.

Add pink food colouring to one bowl and green colouring to another and mix in well. Leave one bowl uncoloured.

Put the three parts of the mixture in separate heaps in a cake tin.

Marble it by dragging a spoon gently through the colours.

Bake in the oven for 40 to 45 minutes.

When it is cool slice it in half with a breadknife and spread one half with jam.

To sift the icing sugar tap the sieve gently with the flat of your hand.

You need this part.

Using the cake tin as a guide to size, draw a simple duck design with a felt-tip pen on greaseproof paper. Cut it out carefully to make a stencil.
   Lay the stencil over the cake. Sift icing sugar thickly over it. Lift the paper off carefully.

Hint
If the greaseproof paper stencil will not lie flat on the cake, brush it with a little water.

7

Jelly baby fun

You will need: bananas, jelly babies, a few grapes, ice cream wafers

knife, plates, child's scissors

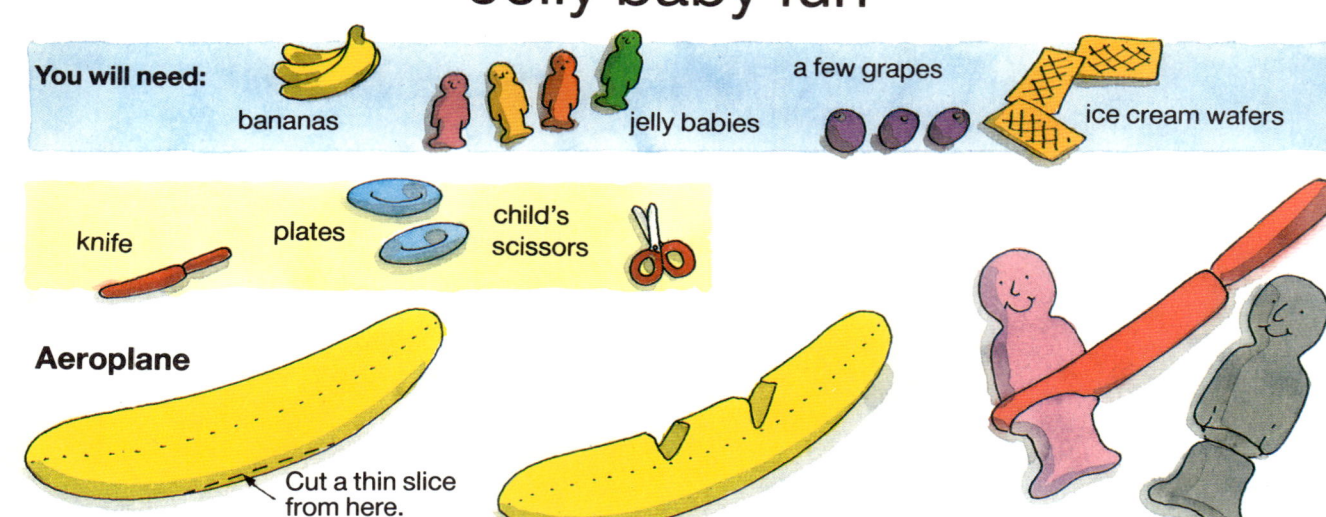

Aeroplane

Cut a thin slice from here.

Peel a long straight banana. Cut a thin slice from one side to prevent it from rolling.

Cut two V-shaped sections from the top to make a cockpit.

Cut two jelly babies in half to make a pilot and a co-pilot.

Trim ice cream wafers with scissors to make wings and fins.

Squirt some cream round the edge of the plate to make exhaust smoke.

Cut a grape in half to make the windscreen.

Cut two slits in which to fit the wings.

Other ideas

Flying saucer
- Scoop of ice cream
- Tinned orange segments
- Jelly baby spacemen on ready-made icing base.
- glacé cherry
- Jelly sweet lights
- Pineapple ring base

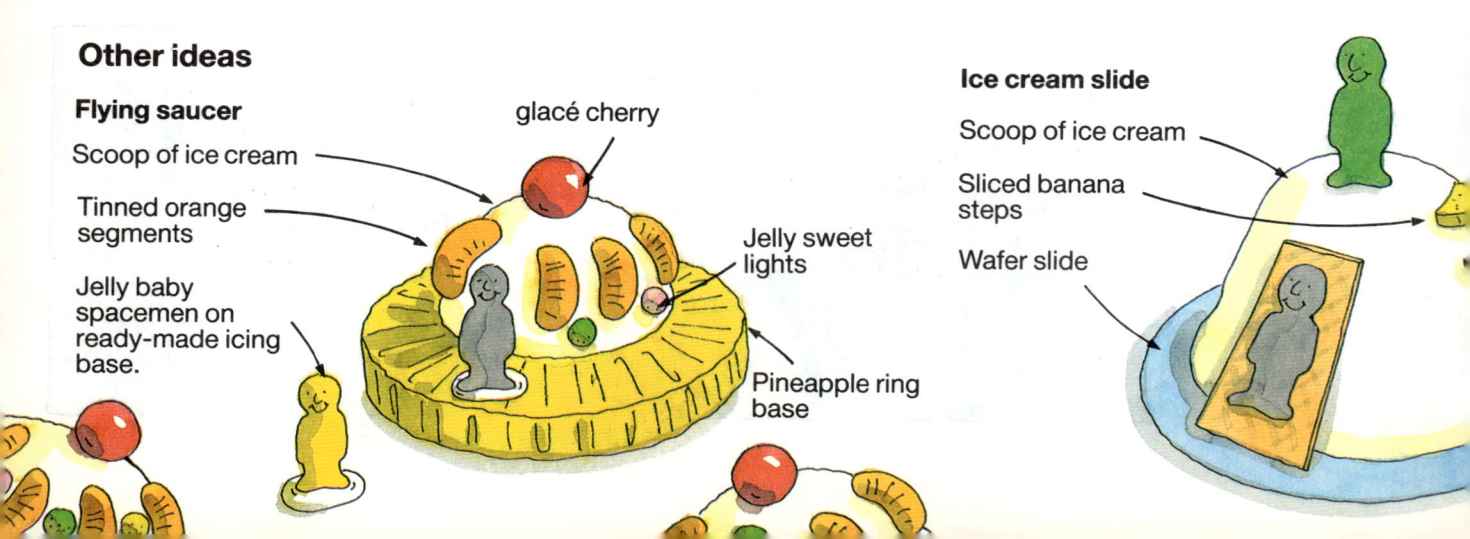

Ice cream slide
- Scoop of ice cream
- Sliced banana steps
- Wafer slide

squirty cream · jelly sweets · jam

Racing car

Place half a peeled banana on a plate. From the other half cut a slice to place behind it.

Cut a V-shaped seat for the driver. Put the top half of a jelly baby in the seat.

Add a quarter of a grape for the windscreen.

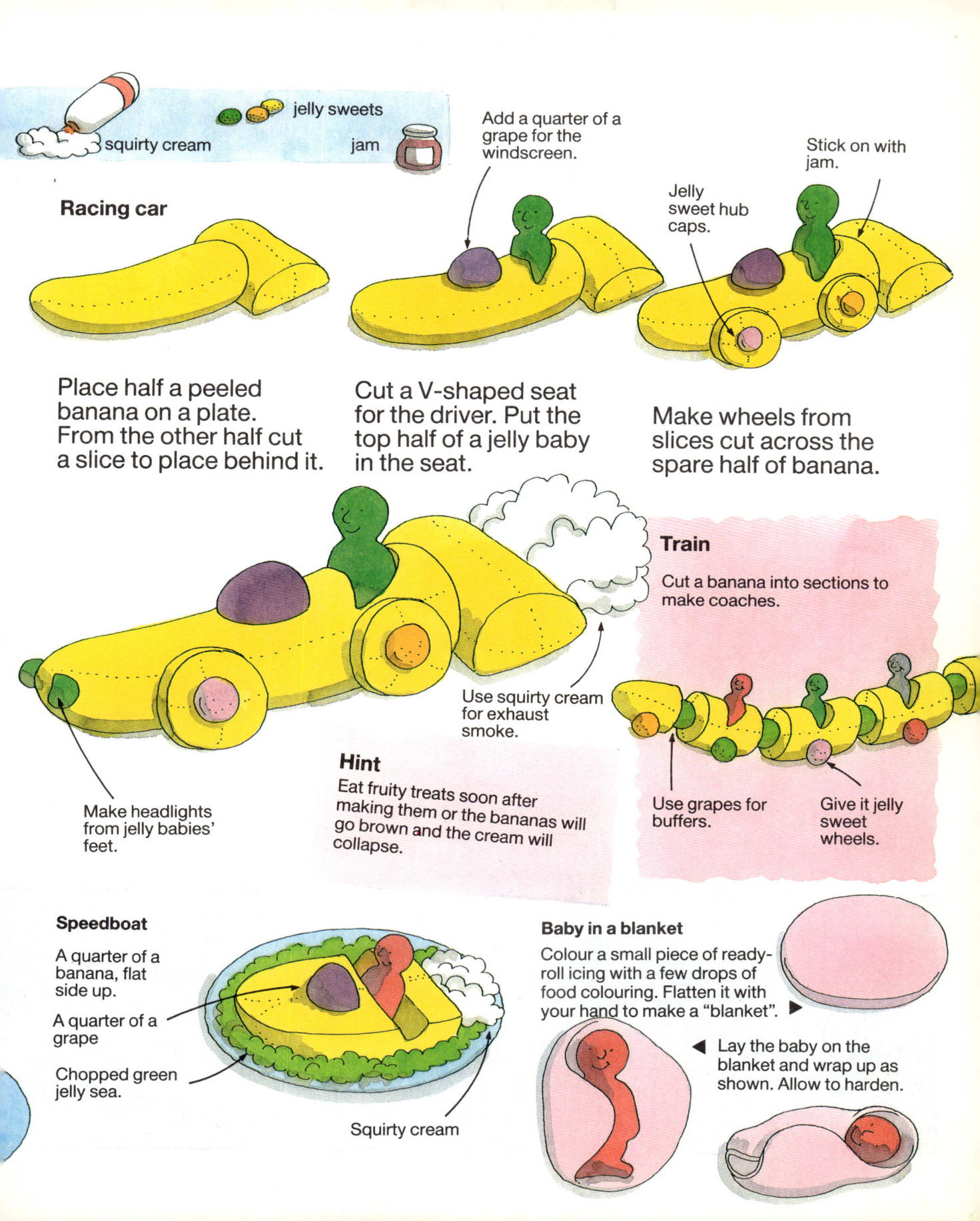

Jelly sweet hub caps.

Stick on with jam.

Make wheels from slices cut across the spare half of banana.

Make headlights from jelly babies' feet.

Use squirty cream for exhaust smoke.

Hint
Eat fruity treats soon after making them or the bananas will go brown and the cream will collapse.

Train
Cut a banana into sections to make coaches.

Use grapes for buffers.

Give it jelly sweet wheels.

Speedboat
- A quarter of a banana, flat side up.
- A quarter of a grape
- Chopped green jelly sea.
- Squirty cream

Baby in a blanket
Colour a small piece of ready-roll icing with a few drops of food colouring. Flatten it with your hand to make a "blanket". ▶

◀ Lay the baby on the blanket and wrap up as shown. Allow to harden.

Flowery hats

You will need: chocolate or plain round biscuits, packet chocolate teacakes (marshmallow biscuits), cold water, icing sugar, jelly diamonds, sugar flowers

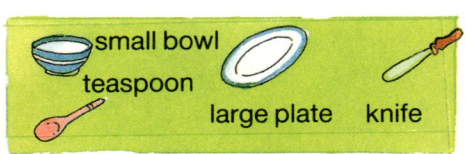

small bowl, teaspoon, large plate, knife

Add a little water to icing sugar to make icing "glue". *Make it quite thick so it doesn't run.*

Spread a little on the centre of each flat biscuit.

Press teacakes gently onto the centre of the biscuits.

Add flowers and jelly diamond "leaves" round the crown. Stick them on with icing glue. Leave to dry.

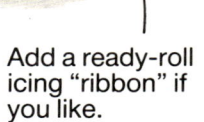

Add a ready-roll icing "ribbon" if you like.

Other ideas

Christmas puddings

Spread a biscuit with coloured icing to make a plate.

Stick a teacake on.

Dribble a little white icing "brandy sauce" over the top.

Add small pieces of jelly diamonds for leaves and holly berries.

Flying saucers

Ice a biscuit. Add a teacake. Sprinkle hundreds and thousands around the edge. Add jelly sweet lights.

Set oven to:
190°C   375°F
Gas mark 5

Bow-tie bears

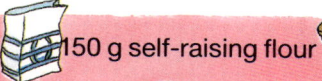

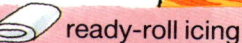

You will need:
- 150 g self-raising flour
- 15 g drinking chocolate
- sultanas
- ready-roll icing
- 100 g margarine
- 50 g castor sugar
- ½ tsp. lemon or vanilla essence
- food colouring
- icing glue (see opposite page)

- electric food mixer
- greased baking tray
- fish-slice
- cooling rack
- small bowl
- rolling-pin
- knife

Combine margarine, flour, sugar and lemon essence in a mixer to make a smooth dough.

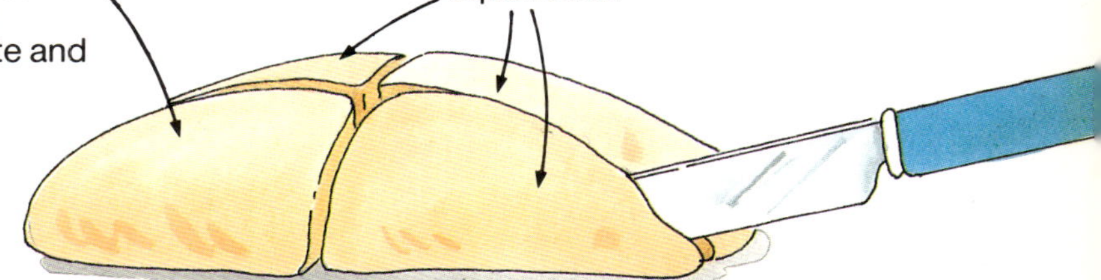

Remove the dough and cut it into four equal parts.

Put one part back in the mixer with drinking chocolate and blend.

Divide each of the other three parts into three to make nine equal balls.

From the remaining ball roll eight small balls for noses. Flatten them and add to the centre of each face.

Flatten balls of chocolate dough onto the faces to make ears.

Add sultanas for eyes and one for nose.

For the bears' faces flatten eight of the balls onto the baking tray with the palm of your hand.

Bake for 12 to 15 minutes in a preheated oven. Allow to cool in the tin for one minute before removing with fish-slice to cool on rack.

Add a bow-tie when cool.

Hints

- Space the biscuits well, as the mixture spreads on cooking.
- If the dough is too crumbly after adding chocolate, add a few drops of milk to bind.
- If you have no food mixer, cream the fat and sugar together, then add the flour. Then continue as above.

Bow-ties

Put a few drops of food colouring in a bowl. Knead in ready-roll icing.

Roll it out. Cut oblongs and pinch in the centre, as shown. Stick on with icing "glue".

11

Set oven to: 230°C 450°F Gas mark 8

Cheesy scones

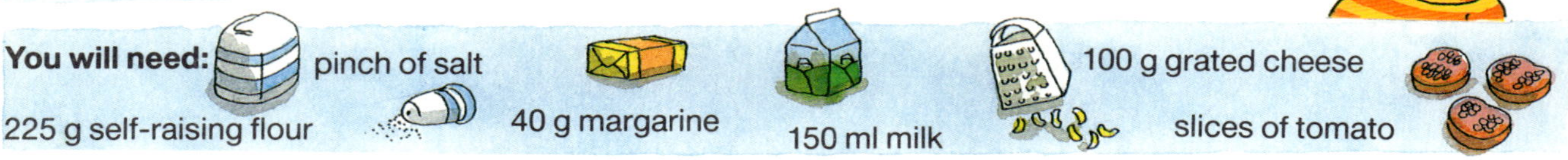

You will need:
- 225 g self-raising flour
- pinch of salt
- 40 g margarine
- 150 ml milk
- 100 g grated cheese
- slices of tomato

- sieve
- large bowl
- rolling-pin
- knife
- scone-cutter (5 cm)
- greased baking tray

Sift flour and salt into large bowl. Cut the margarine up and rub it lightly into the flour.

Flour and margarine mixture should look like fine breadcrumbs.

Stir in half the grated cheese. Add the milk and stir quickly with a knife to mix it in.

Roll the dough on a floured surface.

Push the dough gently together into a ball. Roll it out until it is about 2 cm thick.

Cut out circles with a scone-cutter. Put them on a greased baking sheet.

Sprinkle the rest of the cheese on top and bake for 10 minutes in the preheated oven.

Cut them in half. Fill with sliced tomatoes.

Cheesy twists

Oven: 190°C 375°F Gas mark 5

Roll out some shortcrust pastry thinly. Spread half of it with yeast extract and sprinkle cheese on top.
Fold the other half over the top of the filling.

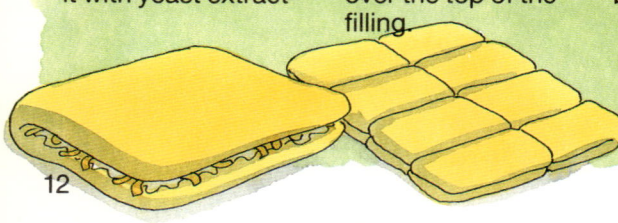

Cut into strips, twist once, and lay on a greased baking tray.

Bake in a preheated oven for 10 to 15 minutes.

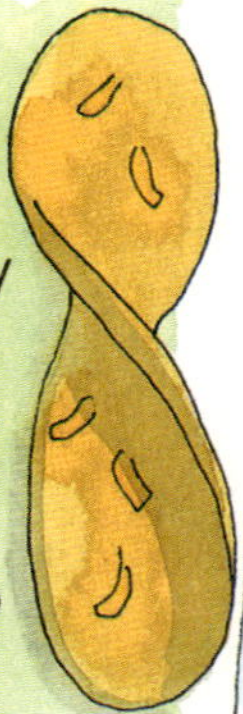

Hints

- Don't handle the dough too much, or it will become tough.

- If the oven is not hot enough the scones may not rise well.

Rice rabbit

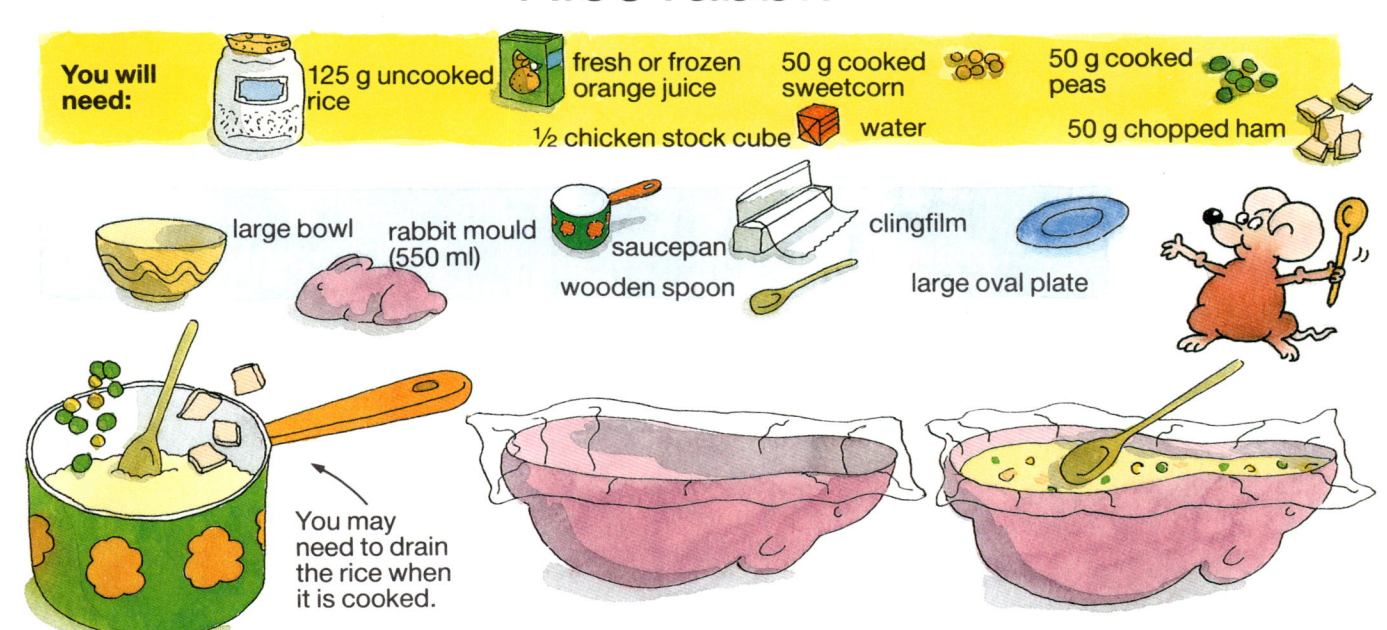

You will need:
- 125 g uncooked rice
- fresh or frozen orange juice
- 50 g cooked sweetcorn
- 50 g cooked peas
- ½ chicken stock cube
- water
- 50 g chopped ham

- large bowl
- rabbit mould (550 ml)
- saucepan
- wooden spoon
- clingfilm
- large oval plate

You may need to drain the rice when it is cooked.

Cook the rice as directed on the packet, using half orange juice and half stock as the cooking liquid. Add ham and vegetables.

Line the mould with clingfilm, pressing it well into all the hollows.

Fill the mould with the rice mixture, pressing it firmly down with the back of a wooden spoon.

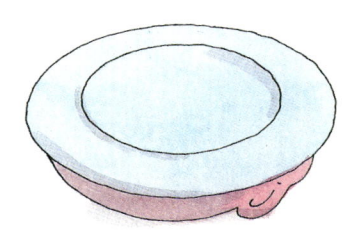

Put the plate over the mould and then turn both the right way up.

Serve with carrot sticks in a section of hollowed out cucumber.

Use shredded lettuce for grass.

Lift the mould off and carefully peel off the clingfilm. Eat warm or cold.

Hints
- Make sure the rice is pressed firmly into ears, nose and tail before filling the rest of the mould.
- You could use cooked celery or broccoli instead of sweetcorn and peas.

Set oven to: 190°C 375°F Gas mark 5

Christmas tree

You will need: mild ginger biscuit dough (see page 32), solid boiled sweets in assorted colours, flour

rolling-pin, non-stick baking parchment, greaseproof paper, felt-tip pen, flat baking tray, scissors, knife, plastic bottle-top or child's small pastry cutters

Use the template opposite to make a greaseproof paper pattern of a Christmas tree.
   Lay some baking parchment over a baking tray.

Roll the ginger biscuit dough out on the parchment until it is about ½ cm thick.

Dust rolling pin with flour.

Lay your pattern over the dough and cut round the outline, using a knife.

Lift the pattern off and carefully peel away the dough from the edges.

Use a straw to press out a small hole at the top.

Cut shapes out of the dough tree, using a bottle-top or child's pastry cutters.

Bake in a preheated oven for 10 minutes. Take it out of the oven, place a boiled sweet in each cut-out shape and bake for a further five minutes.

wool or fine ribbon

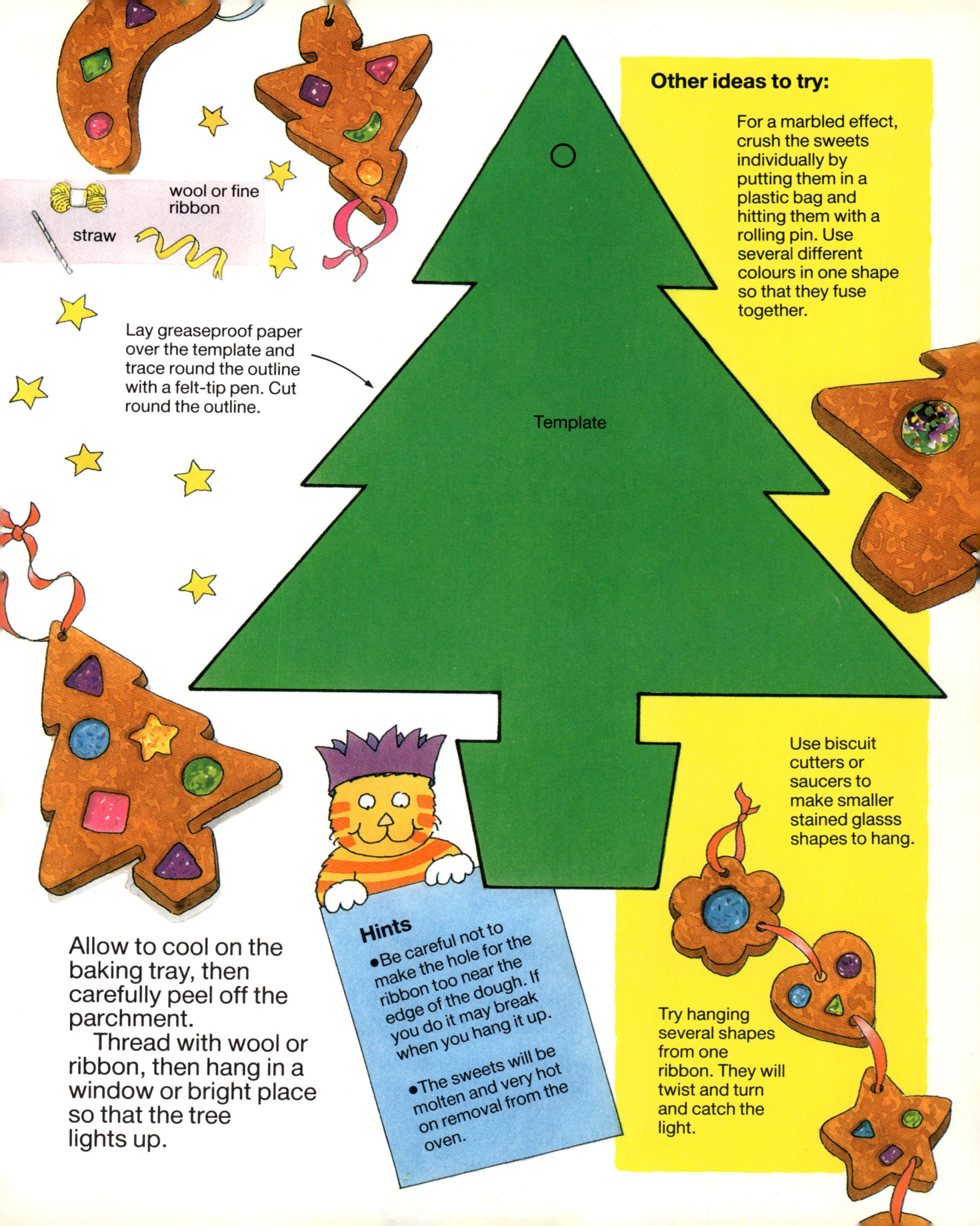

straw

Lay greaseproof paper over the template and trace round the outline with a felt-tip pen. Cut round the outline.

Template

Other ideas to try:

For a marbled effect, crush the sweets individually by putting them in a plastic bag and hitting them with a rolling pin. Use several different colours in one shape so that they fuse together.

Use biscuit cutters or saucers to make smaller stained glasss shapes to hang.

Allow to cool on the baking tray, then carefully peel off the parchment.

Thread with wool or ribbon, then hang in a window or bright place so that the tree lights up.

Hints
- Be careful not to make the hole for the ribbon too near the edge of the dough. If you do it may break when you hang it up.
- The sweets will be molten and very hot on removal from the oven.

Try hanging several shapes from one ribbon. They will twist and turn and catch the light.

Cress creatures

You will need: cress seeds, jug of cold water, brown or black felt or paper, scissors, potatoes, dinner plate, scrap of white felt or paper

Woolly sheep

Tease some cotton wool into a rough oblong shape for the body and lay it on a plate.

Cut some ears, a face and some legs out of black felt and lay them on the cotton wool.

Cut the eyes out of white felt and mark in the centre with a felt-tip pen.

Add some extra cotton wool for the forehead and tail.

Water cotton wool thoroughly.

Sprinkle some cress seeds over the cotton wool.

Don't sprinkle the seeds too thickly.

Keep the cotton wool moist by pouring a little water onto the plate each day.

In a few days the sheep's fleece will be ready to shear with scissors and eat.

Ideas for eating your cress

With cottage cheese or cream cheese in sandwiches.

With egg in sandwiches.

As a garnish for sliced tomatoes or cucumbers.

As a filling in hot buttered scones (see page 12).

As a topping for baked potatoes with cream cheese or chopped grilled bacon.

16

cotton wool — black felt-tip pen — carrot — potato peeler

Hairy caterpillar

Cut some bits of carrot to fit in the eyes, nose and mouth.

Scrub some potatoes. Choose a small one for the head and cut out a face with a potato peeler.

Slice the tops off the other potatoes. Scoop some of the potato out and replace it with cotton wool.

Water the cotton wool and sprinkle it with seeds.

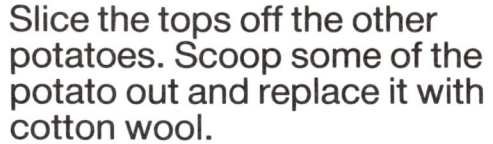

Arrange the potatoes in order of size behind the head. Watch the caterpillar get hairier and hairier.

Clown

Cut a slice from the base of a potato so it will stand. Cut out a face and insert a carrot-stick nose. Grow some hair on top.

Add pieces of potatoe for feet.

Other ideas to try:

Lion
Use orange felt and a frayed wool tail. Give him a cotton wool mane.

Stencils
Place a shaped biscuit cutter on cotton wool. Sprinkle seeds evenly inside them carefully remove cutter.

Names

Tease some cotton wool into fat strings and arrange in letter shapes on a plate.

Hedgehog
Find a potato with a pointed end for a nose. Cut out some eyes. Grow prickles on his back.

17

Hallowe'en lantern

You will need: large, ripe melon; orange crêpe paper; old newspaper; dessertspoon; two bowls; kitchen roll; sharp knife*; string; potato peeler; small torch

Newspaper will stop your working surface from getting sticky.

Spread out some newspaper and put the melon on it. Slice off the most pointed end with a sharp knife.

Scoop the seeds out into a bowl. Scoop the flesh from the melon and the lid into another bowl, leaving a shell about 1 cm thick.

Cut out some eyes, a nose and a mouth, using a sharp knife.* Make some holes to thread a string handle through, using a potato peeler.

Turn the melon upside down and allow to drain for a few minutes. Use kitchen towel to pat the inside as dry as possible.

Line the inside with crêpe paper, covering the cut out shapes and pressing it against the sides. Thread string through the holes.

Switch on a small torch. Place it inside the melon, so the light shines through the crêpe paper. Put the lid on.

For safety you could put a cork on the end when not in use.

Set oven to: 190°C 375°F Gas mark 5

Easter nests

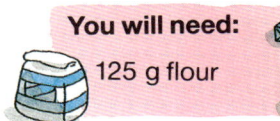

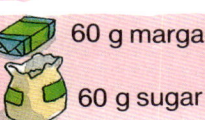

You will need:
- 125 g flour
- 60 g margarine
- 60 g sugar
- ½ small beaten egg
- mixed spice
- food colouring
- ready-roll icing or white marzipan

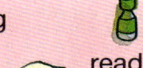

large mixing bowl, wooden spoon, sieve, garlic press, rolling pin, 6cm scone cutter, flat baking tray, plate

Make a quantity of biscuit dough*. Roll out ½cm thick on a flat baking tray.

Cut 6 rounds, evenly spaced with a 6cm scone cutter. Remove the excess dough very carefully.

Squeeze the excess dough through a garlic press. Catch the strings of dough on a plate.

Lay twisted strings of dough round the edges of your rounds to make nests.

You could buy candy or chocolate eggs to fill your nests.

Bake for 15-17 minutes in a pre-heated oven until golden.

When cool, fill with eggs made from marzipan or icing with a little food colouring kneaded into it.

*See page 32 for recipe, substituting mixed spice for ginger.

Giant stripey bees

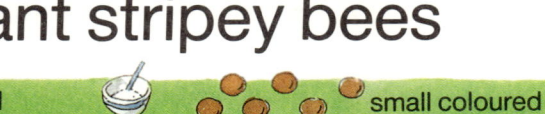

You will need:
- 1 plain swiss roll
- 1 chocolate swiss roll
- a little stiff icing and water for glue
- chocolate buttons
- small coloured chocolate sweets

- rice paper or greaseproof paper
- pencil
- large plate
- scissors
- knife
- green paper

Divide each swiss roll into three, then divide each third into three to make nine slices per cake.

Each bee will need three slices from each cake. Sandwich alternate colours together with icing and water "glue."

Stick on chocolate sweet eyes.

Press a chocolate button sideways into each end for a nose and tail.

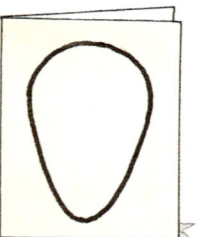

Draw and cut a pair of wings from folded paper.

For a party you could decorate the plate with green paper leaves.

Ease spaces between the second and third slices with a knife to insert wings. Arrange bees on a large plate.

Other ideas to try:

Owl
- Turn a slice on its end for the head.
- Use half slices for the wings.
- Use jelly diamonds for ears, beak and feet.

Butterfly
Decorate the wings with coloured sweets and jelly diamonds.

You could make the owl and the butterfly with only one colour of cake.

Set oven to: 190°C 375°F Gas mark 5

Pink sunset pudding

You will need:
- grated rind and juice of 2 lemons
- 2 eggs separated
- red food colouring
- 1 tin condensed milk (400 ml)
- 100 g castor sugar

- 2 large bowls
- tin opener
- wooden spoon
- ovenproof flan dish (approx. 23 cm)
- electric whisk
- large metal spoon
- knife

Mix together the lemon juice and rind, egg yolks, condensed milk and a few drops of red food colouring.

In another bowl whisk the egg whites with a few drops of food colouring until stiff.

Whisk in half the sugar, then fold in the remaining sugar using a metal spoon.

Pour the milk mixture into a flan dish. Spoon the egg whites on top.

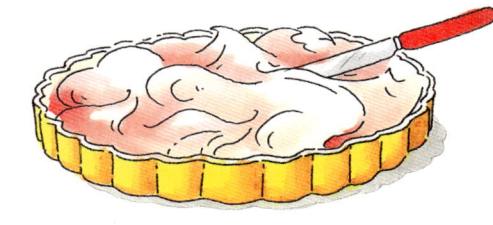

Flick into swirls and peaks using the knife.

Hints

- Make sure the bowl for the egg whites is dry and completely free of grease.
- This pudding tastes even better the day after you have made it.
- It can be used as a filling in a shortcrust pastry case, which has been baked blind for 10 minutes.

Bake for 12 to 15 minutes until crisp and lightly browned. Eat warm or cold.

Ham, cheese and pineapple slices

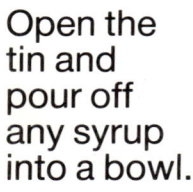

You will need:
- butter for spreading
- 4 slices thin-cut ham
- 4 tinned pineapple rings
- 4 slices processed cheese
- 4 small slices of bread
- butterfly-type tin opener
- kitchen roll
- small bowl
- butter knife
- fish-slice

Press firmly on the bottom of the tin.

Open the tin and pour off any syrup into a bowl.

Use kitchen roll to pat the pineapple dry.

Using the tin as a cutter, press out four circles each from the bread, ham and cheese slices.

Toast the bread lightly on both sides under a grill, then butter it on one side.

Put a circle of ham, then pineapple on each round of bread, then top with cheese.

Using a fish-slice replace under the grill and heat until the cheese is melted and bubbling.

Hint

Use up any scraps of bread to make breadcrumbs in a blender. Use them for a savoury crumble topping or stuffing, or freeze them for later use.

Pretend pizzas

Toast some circles of bread, as above. Spread with a little tomato paste.

Sprinkle sliced vegetables and scraps of ham, salami or tuna on top.

Top with cheese and sprinkle sparingly with dried herbs. Place under the grill.

22

Hedgehog nibbles

You will need: a little milk, carrot sticks, cucumber slices, cream cheese, crisps, savoury stick biscuits, sultanas

large plate, wooden spoon, bowl, tea-towel

Rest the bowl on a tea-towel to prevent it slipping.

Beat the cream cheese with a little milk to soften it.

Put the cheese on a plate and pat it into a pear-shape with the wooden spoon.

Add sultana eyes and noses.

Press in vegetables, crisps, or savoury stick biscuits to make the hedgehog's prickles.

Hints

- You can make pink hedgehogs by adding a little tomato ketchup to the cheese.

- Try sweet hedgehogs, using pieces of tinned or fresh fruit for prickles.

Faces

Use a selection of sliced, shredded or chopped vegetables to create faces on bread circles (or rolls cut in half) spread with butter or cheese spread.

Sultana, Carrot, Cucumber, Radish, Cheese, Apple, Sweetcorn, Pepper

23

Dreamy drinks

Milk shakes

Whisk the ingredients together in a tall jug, using a hand whisk. Or use an electric blender, but don't remove the lid until the machine has completely stopped.

Use wide straws for thick shakes. If you want thinner shakes reduce the amount of ice cream and add ice cubes.

The amounts given will make enough for one adult and two children.

Vanilla

Top with squirty cream and a glacé cherry.

Chocolate

Top with squirty cream and grated chocolate or chocolate vermicelli.

Hint

Save the juice from cans of fruit to make refreshing drinks. Dilute with water, fruit juices or lemonade.

You will need:

300 ml milk

4 tablespoons vanilla ice cream

¼ teaspoon vanilla essence

300 ml milk

4 tablespoons chocolate ice cream

1 tablespoon chocolate dessert syrup

Other ideas to try:

Orange yoghurt drink

300 ml natural yoghurt

juice of 2 oranges

2 to 3 tablespoons runny honey

Blend together as for milk shakes. Decorate with a slice of orange.

Ice cream soda

Fill a tall glass two thirds full of lemonade, or your favourite fizzy drink.
Add one or two scoops of ice cream and stir with a long spoon.

Strawberry

Top with tinned or sliced fresh strawberries.

Blackcurrant

Banana

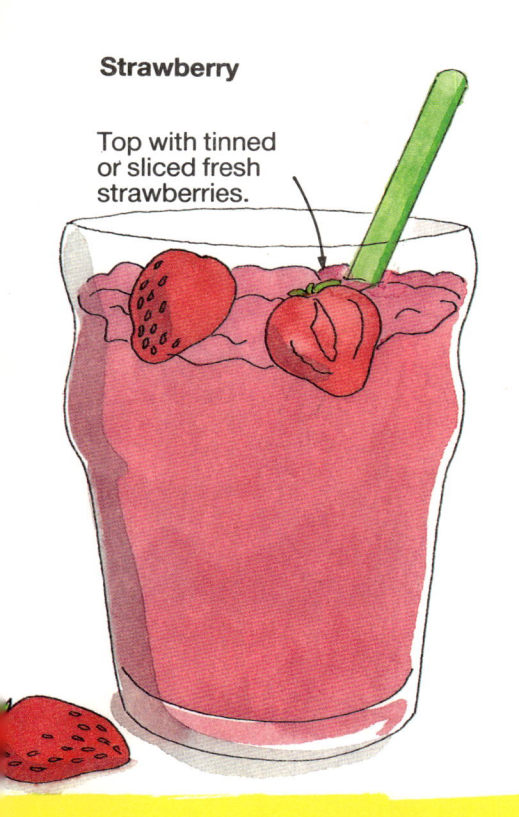

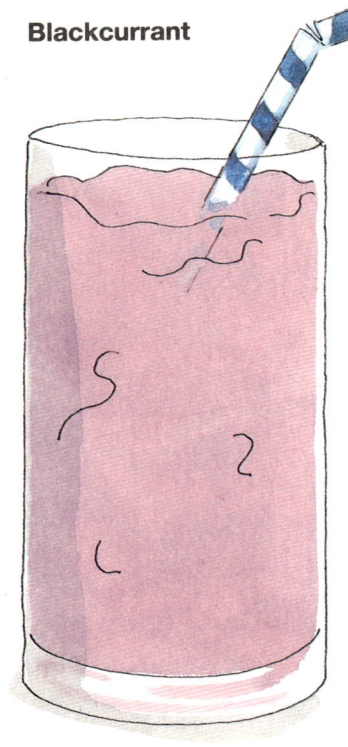

300 ml milk

150 ml strawberry yoghurt

3 tablespoons strawberry ice cream

300 ml milk

6 tablespoons vanilla ice cream

3 tablespoons blackcurrant concentrate

1 ripe banana

300 ml milk

4 tablespoons vanilla ice cream

2 teaspoons honey

Squashy orange

Roll, squeeze and pinch a thin-skinned orange until it feels very soft all over.
Chill it, if you like, then poke a hole near the top with a potato peeler. Insert a short piece of straw and then drink.

Fun with ice cubes

Try freezing pieces of fruit, mint leaves, rose petals in ice to make decorative ice cubes, or freeze fruit juices to liven up drinks of squash.

Microwave castles

You will need:
- 140 g self-raising flour
- ½ tsp. baking-powder
- 75 g butter
- 60 g soft brown sugar
- 1 egg, beaten
- ¾ can blackcurrant pie filling
- 1½ tbsp. milk
- squirty cream

- 6 paper cups*
- wooden spoon
- large plate
- large bowl
- large metal spoon
- knife

Cut up the butter and rub it into the flour and baking powder. Mix in the sugar.

Mix in the egg and milk and half the tin of fruit pie-filling.

Stand the cups in a circle on a plate.

Put half a tablespoonful of fruit pie-filling into the bottom of each paper cup.

Fill each cup with the flour mixture until about half full.

Put in a microwave** oven. Cook on "high", turning once, for about four minutes. Stand for one minute.

Hint
Use up leftover pie-filling as a hot sauce for ice cream. Heat it in the microwave.

Turn out the castles, then decorate with squirty cream.

*Don't use plastic cups. Some plastics give off dangerous fumes
**Do not use an ordinary oven.

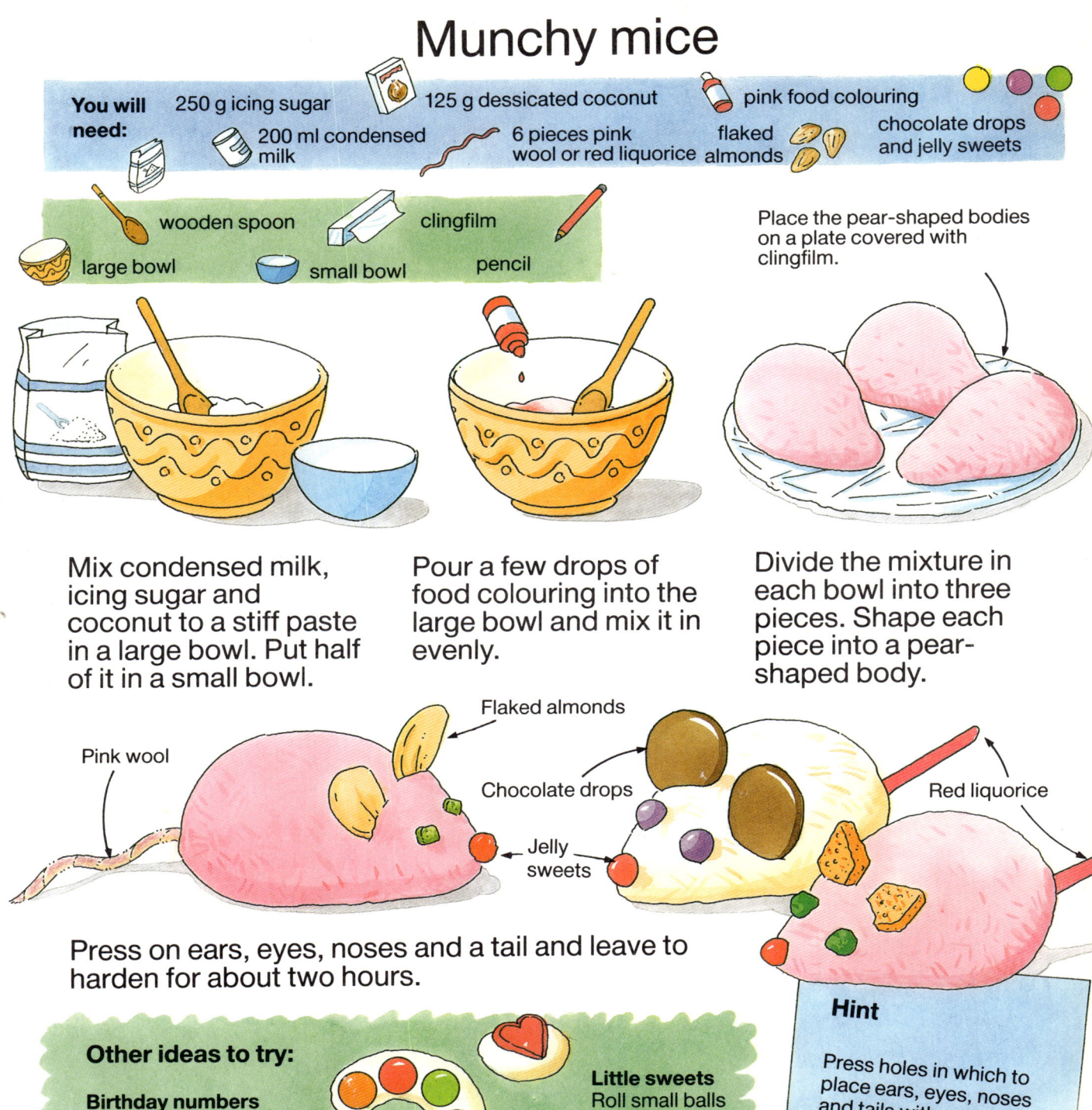

Munchy mice

You will need:
- 250 g icing sugar
- 200 ml condensed milk
- 125 g dessicated coconut
- 6 pieces pink wool or red liquorice
- pink food colouring
- flaked almonds
- chocolate drops and jelly sweets

- wooden spoon
- clingfilm
- large bowl
- small bowl
- pencil

Mix condensed milk, icing sugar and coconut to a stiff paste in a large bowl. Put half of it in a small bowl.

Pour a few drops of food colouring into the large bowl and mix it in evenly.

Place the pear-shaped bodies on a plate covered with clingfilm.

Divide the mixture in each bowl into three pieces. Shape each piece into a pear-shaped body.

Press on ears, eyes, noses and a tail and leave to harden for about two hours.

Labels: Pink wool, Flaked almonds, Chocolate drops, Jelly sweets, Red liquorice

Other ideas to try:

Birthday numbers
Draw a large number on greaseproof paper and cover it with clingfilm.
Use this as a pattern on which to place Munchy Mice mixture. Press small sweets on top to decorate.

Little sweets
Roll small balls of the mixture and press a sweet onto the top of each one.

Hint

Press holes in which to place ears, eyes, noses and tails with a pencil covered with clingfilm. This will help them to stick. Or you could use jam or icing sugar and water to glue them in position.

Ice cream cake surprise

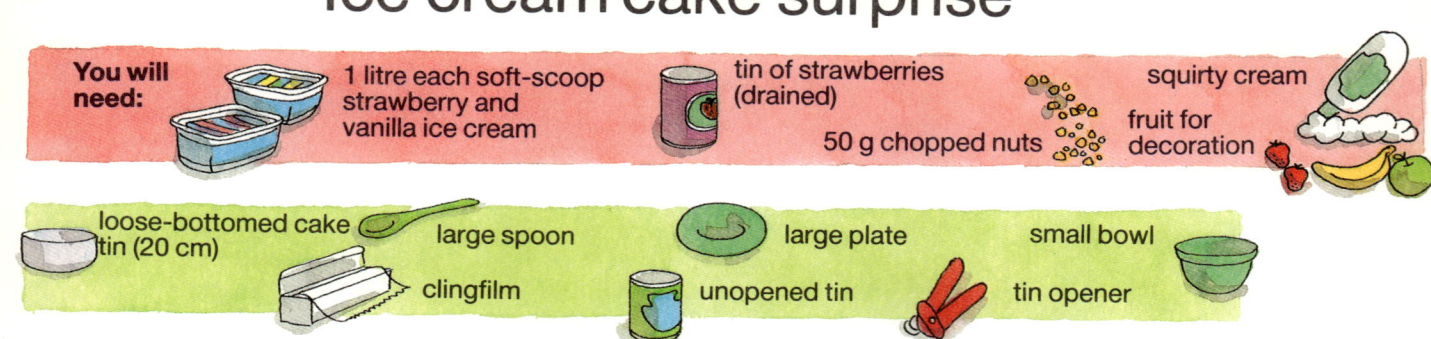

You will need: 1 litre each soft-scoop strawberry and vanilla ice cream • tin of strawberries (drained) • 50 g chopped nuts • squirty cream • fruit for decoration

loose-bottomed cake tin (20 cm) • large spoon • large plate • small bowl • clingfilm • unopened tin • tin opener

Line the cake tin with clingfilm. Sprinkle chopped nuts to cover the base.

For those who don't like nuts use crushed biscuits.

Cover the nuts with alternate scoops of pink and white ice cream. Press down well.

Using a spoon, scoop some ice cream out of the centre into a small bowl.

Don't scoop right to the bottom.

Pour drained fruit into the hollow, almost to the top.

Replace the scooped out ice cream over the top. Freeze until firm.

Smooth over using back of spoon.

28

Press cake tin down onto can.

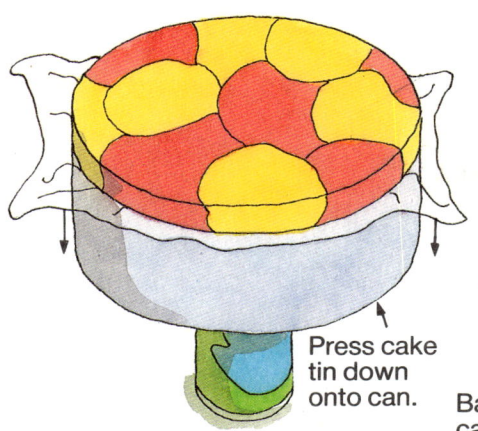

Base of cake tin.

To remove the cake from its mould, press the bottom of the cake tin on to a tin can.

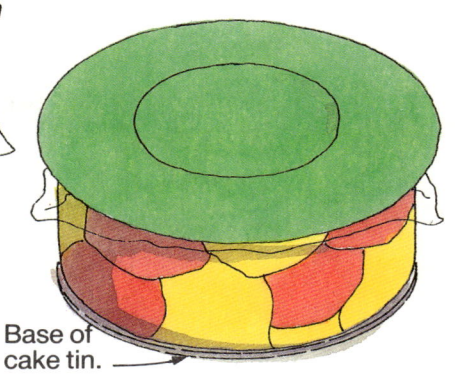

Put a plate on top, turn it over and remove the cake tin base and clingfilm.

Decorate with squirty cream and fruit.

Allow it to soften for about 30 minutes. Cut as required.

Hints
- Use oven gloves when handling frozen tins to avoid freezer burn.
- To cut ice cream use a knife dipped in hot water.
- To get ice cream out of a mould, dip the mould very briefly into hot water.
- You can add crushed meringues to the ice cream if you like.

Other ideas to try:

Wafer surprise

Lay a slice of ice cream on a wafer. Press into it a selection of the following:

jelly sweets

slices of tinned or fresh fruit

chocolate buttons

Press on a second wafer lid and freeze until firm

Jelly-mould ice creams

Use small jelly moulds lined with clingfilm as ice cream moulds. Press down firmly into all corners.

29

Banana lollies

You will need: firm bananas, runny honey, chopped nuts

new or sterilized lolly sticks, 2 large plates, clingfilm, saucer, knife, pastry brush

Pour some honey into a saucer and nuts onto a plate.

Insert a clean lolly stick into half a peeled banana. Brush it with honey.

Roll the banana in the nuts until it is covered. Sprinkle more over if necessary.

Arrange on a plate covered with clingfilm and then freeze.

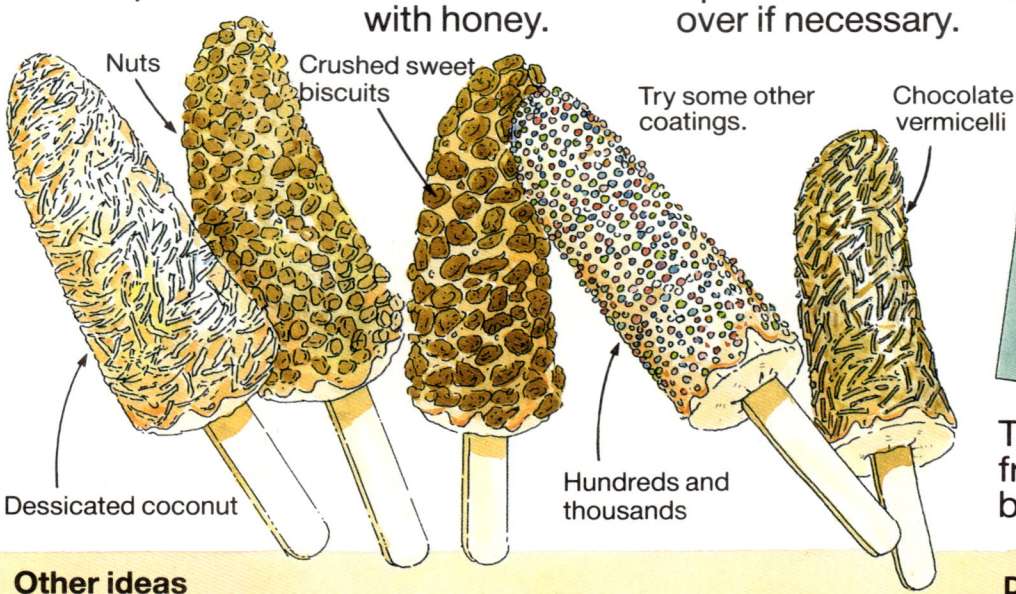

Nuts — Crushed sweet biscuits — Try some other coatings. — Chocolate vermicelli

Dessicated coconut — Hundreds and thousands

Hints
- If the honey is too stiff, warm the jar (without its lid) in the microwave for a few seconds, or in hot water.
- You can use the handle end of plastic spoons if you haven't got any lolly sticks.

Take out of freezer 2 hours before eating.

Other ideas

Yoghurt melties

3 tablespoons frozen orange juice (unthawed)
6 tablespoons natural yoghurt
caster sugar to taste
3 tablespoons water

Mix all the ingredients together until mushy.

Pour into an ice-cube tray or the moulded plastic tray from a chocolate box.

Freeze. Turn out as needed.

Fruit lollies

Freeze fruit squash or the syrup from tinned fruit.

Don't forget to add sticks before freezing.

Drip-free lollies

When quite cool pour liquid jelly into small moulds such as egg cups or ice-cube trays.

Try layers of jelly and cooled custard or banana mashed with strawberry jam.

Parents' notes

Getting prepared

It is worth spending time on careful preparation before you start cooking to make things go smoothly. Get children into good kitchen habits from the start.

● Start by putting on aprons and washing hands.

● Clear a surface so that you have plenty of space to work on and show children how to wipe it down well.

● Gather all the ingredients and utensils before you begin and check them off together from the panels at the top of the pages.

● Prop up this book so that you can see your chosen page carefully. A cook's bookstand is ideal for doing this.

● To make clearing up easier put some old newspapers on the floor.

● If you will need the oven, set it to the right temperature before you begin.

Weighing and measuring

● It is a good idea to spoon dry ingredients onto scales rather than pouring them from a packet. There will be more control and less spillage.

● Instead of scales you could use a measuring jug, which shows levels for dry ingredients as well as liquids.

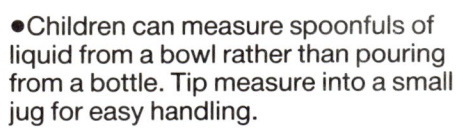

● Stand jugs and liquids on a tray. Drips and dribbles won't run all over your work area and need immediate clearing up.

● Children can measure spoonfuls of liquid from a bowl rather than pouring from a bottle. Tip measure into a small jug for easy handling.

Utensils

Jugs: Use plastic jugs for measuring or pouring wherever possible. They are safer and light to handle.

Bowls: should always be the right size for the job: egg-whites can quadruple in volume; flour and icing sugar can drift in clouds from a small bowl; china bowls hold steady for mixing and whisking. Small plastic bowls are easy to handle when adding other ingredients.
  To avoid slipping stand bowls on a tea towel while creaming and mixing. Small bowls are useful to take discarded egg shells.
  Put used cutlery blade end down into mugs.

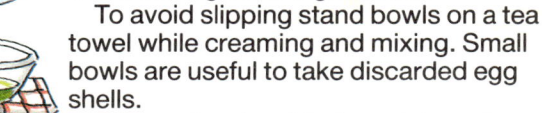

Knives: Use round-ended knives wherever possible. If you need to use a sharp knife, put a piece of cork on the tip when not in use.

Tinopeners: Use the "butterfly" type if possible – they do not leave a ragged edge on the tin. Wrap lids carefully in double newspaper and discard immediately. To drain the contents of a tin pour slowly into a sieve over a bowl at least as wide.

Cutters: use plastic cutters. Metal ones are sharp and could be pressed into dough upside down by mistake, hurting a child's hand. You can also use plastic tumblers, washed aerosol caps etc. for cutting out shapes.

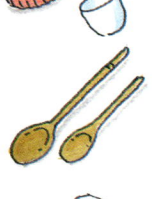

Wooden spoons: come in different lengths, choose a short one for a child's use.

Food graters: plastic ones are safer than metal. Grating is quite hard work and children may tire of it quickly. Take over yourself when the item becomes too small to handle safely.

Electrical gadgets

These are great time and effort savers and there is no reason why a small child should not help use them with careful supervision. Never leave an appliance plugged in and unattended. Keep them well away from sinks and bowls of liquid.

Food processors: make sure the machine has completely stopped, before taking off the lid and removing the contents.

Egg whisks: use a high-sided bowl. For safety and to avoid the mixture flying off, switch beaters on and off while blades are inside the bowl.

Ovens

- Make sure that children are well aware of the dangers of a hot oven. Make an obvious show of wearing oven gloves even while just checking baking progress – the door and door knobs on some ovens can become quite hot.
- Ask small children to stand well back from an oven. There could be a blast of hot air in their face and they shouldn't get underfoot while you deal with hot food.
- Check that you have a clear heatproof space ready to take a hot dish before you you open up the oven.
- Use a fish slice for transferring food safely to a cooling rack.
- Some foods need to be cooled in the baking tray but make sure you place them well out of reach.

Freezers

Use oven gloves to avoid freezer burn, especially from metal containers such as cake-tins and ice-cube trays.

Microwave ovens

Be careful to stress that in some cases the container might be cool, but the contents very hot. Paper containers will feel very hot to the touch as the heat of the food comes through.

When using clingfilm in the microwave make sure it is the non-toxic kind especially for microwave use.

Foods

Flour: the recipes in this book use white flour. Other flours can be used, but may require more liquid to achieve the right consistency.

Food colourings: if you are worried about the effect of these additives, you can get non-artificial food colourings from health food stores.

Extend your range of colours by mixing various combinations before adding to the food.

To colour ready-roll icing put a few drops of colouring in a bowl and knead the required amount of icing into it until the colour is even. If the colouring makes the icing too wet, sift a little icing sugar into it and knead it in.

To colour ordinary icing make up the icing slightly stiffer than needed, then add the drops of colour a little at a time until the right colour and consistency is reached.

Mild ginger biscuit dough

125 g plain flour
60 g margarine
60 g brown sugar
½ a small beaten egg
1 tsp ground ginger

- Beat the margarine and sugar together until creamy.
- Add the egg, a little at a time.
- Sift in the flour and ginger.
- Mix well to make a firm dough.
If it is too soft add a little more flour.

Victoria sandwich cake mix

100 g margarine
100 g castor sugar
100 g self-raising flour
2 eggs

- Cream the margarine and sugar together until light and fluffy.
- Beat in the eggs gradually, adding a little flour each time to prevent curdling.
- Fold in the rest of the flour.